Upfront:

An Entrepreneur's Quick Start Guide

By Dr. Terré Holmes Arnold
Carla Jones, MBA
Angel Radcliffe, MBA

Copyright © 2016

All rights reserved. No part of this book shall be reproduced, stored in a retrieval system or transmitted by any means, electronic, mechanical, photocopying, recording, or otherwise, without written permission from the publisher.

No patent liability is assumed with respect to the use of information contained herein. Although every precaution has been taken in the preparation of this book, the publisher and authors assume no responsibility for errors or omissions, neither is any liability assumed for damages resulting from the use of information contained herein.

This publication contains the opinions and ideas of the authors. It is intended to provide helpful and informative material on the subject matter covered.

The authors and publisher specifically disclaim any responsibility for any liability, loss, or risk, personal or otherwise, which is incurred as a consequence, directly or indirectly, of the use and application of any of the contents of this book.

Upfront: An Entrepreneur's Quick Start Guide
by Dr. Terré Holmes Arnold
Carla Jones, MBA
Angel Radcliffe, MBA

Copyright © 2016

ISBN-13: 978-1539074168
ISBN-10: 1539074161

Contact info:

UPFRONTBIZ@GMAIL.COM

Direct inquires and/or orders to the above email address.

All rights reserved. Except for use in a review no portion of this book may be reproduced in any form without the express written permission of the publisher.

Neither the authors, company, editor nor the publisher assumes responsibility for the use or misuse of information contained in this book.

What the readers are saying

"As a brand-new entrepreneur, you need a plan; 'Upfront' gives you a step by step formula to succeed. In one sitting you have the ability to create your own strategy in the four most important aspects of starting a business; formation, finance, technology & branding. This is one source I definitely recommend for your preparation of entrepreneurial success."

Raynold Fabre-Jeune
Owner, Downright Entertainment Enterprises, LLC

"*Upfront An Entrepreneur's Quick Start Guide* reads like a 'playbook'. The information was practical, informative, easy to understand, and certainly a value-add."

Cameron Shaw
CEO, End State Business Solutions, LLC

"Proper planning and starting your new business off right in the early phases can save time, money, and unnecessary labor in the wrong places. Upfront: An Entrepreneur's Quick Start Guide provides entrepreneurs everything they need to start their business. Moreover, the authors laid out questions for the reader to ask themselves to ensure they understand the processes."

Dr. Tywanda D. Tate
CEO, Prosperity Business Solutions Group, LLC

TABLE OF CONTENTS

What the Readers Are Saying	*IV*
Introduction	*VI*
Meet the Authors	*IX*
Legitimizing Your Business	*1*
Building Business Credit	*13*
Apps You Need In Business	*25*
Building a Badass Brand	*31*
Sealing the Deal with Clients	*45*
Collaborating with Any Team	*59*
Appendix	*73*
New Business Owner Checklist	*75*
New Small Business Questionnaire	*78*
Building A Badass Brand Worksheets	*90*
Index	*102*

INTRODUCTION

What do you get when you take three business professionals with three specific industry areas of expertise and combined perspectives for the business owner? You guessed it, *Upfront: An Entrepreneurs Quick Start Guide*.

Just as a structure is built on a solid foundation, so are the guiding principles that support business success. As a professional collaborative, Angel, Carla, and Terré have combined their specific areas of expertise and provided the fundamental information that most business owners struggle with. While many have dreams of business ownership, the truth is that most don't take the necessary steps upfront to ensure their business success from the beginning.

Having a great idea supported by those who don't have the knowledge or experience to ensure your success plagues many who venture into business ownership, growth or expansion.

Upfront: An Entrepreneurs Quick Start Guide looks at the basic business fundamentals in four key areas that most business owners struggle with, new or experienced. *Upfront* focuses on business start-up activities, what is required to protect your brand, the how and why to attracting your ideal clients, customer or core user and the fundamentals required around business finance.

Upfront, makes it simple, quick, easy and informative. By breaking down the most important areas of business start-up or expansion into digestible, clear bite size pieces, the reader will gain not only the insight needed but direction on what, where, and how. Each of the six chapters delivers the information in a 'five easy steps' format.

If you have been challenged with gaining clarity and business direction, the struggle is over. *Upfront*, is your roadmap to ensure your journey to business success as an entrepreneur is concise, directional, and achievable.

Through this guide, each contributor provides the support and the path by which to journey and they don't make it hard, lengthy, or confusing.

You've waited long enough. Ready. Set. Go. There is no better time than now to get started.

Meet the Authors

x

Dr. Terré is a Human Development Specialist with over 20 years of experience working with young people and adults on personal empowerment. Over the past two decades she has held leadership roles in both the non-profit and for-profit sectors and has started several successful businesses of her own, including her former company, **DramaSmarts**, where she sent teaching artists into schools to teach reading, writing, and speaking skills through the arts.

She currently runs **EnvisionU, LLC**, a human development firm, where she offers personal and professional development courses and workshops focused on women empowerment, healing, and life transformation.

Terré is an international educator, three-time published author, transformational speaker, certified life coach, serial-preneur, and a mentor to other women, as well as a master teacher and facilitator.

You may connect with **Terré** below:

FACEBOOK: facebook.com/terreholmesspeaks
FACEBOOK GROUP: bitly.com/wewomennetwork
IG/Twitter/Periscope: @terreholmes
WEB: www.terreholmes.com
EMAIL: info@terreholmes.com
LINKEDIN: www.linkedin.com/in/terreholmes

Carla Jones, MBA is a Health and Beauty Industry Influencer performing "money makeover" artistry for beauty and barber industry professionals. After master performances at power houses that include L'Oréal, Revlon, General Motors, Pfizer Pharmaceuticals and Empire Education Group, Carla Jones is showing beauty and barber professionals how to connect their distinctive style with revenue and profitability for their businesses. Carla Jones has been charged with driving revenue in every corporate position she's held, and this licensed industry professional has accomplished exactly that across multiple industries. Companies have been tapping into her thought leadership on revenue generation, cost cutting, and consumer trends for nearly three decades. Intermingled with countless recognitions for innovative new approaches that increased business efficiencies and identified revenue opportunities for corporations, she's also an award-winning stylist.

Carla Jones leverages her expertise and proprietary business tools (GPS - Gross Profit Strategies) to assist beauty and barber professionals in driving predictable revenue and morph into *highly compensated* entrepreneurs. Online digital and social media marketing strategies are the color mix of her edgy brand. She understands that the beauty and barber industry professional must consistently generate profits to live the lives they love and run successful businesses they dream of.

You may connect with **Carla** below:

FACEBOOK: fb.com/salonsolutionsgroup
FACEBOOK GROUP: bit.ly/joinwecre8te
IG/Twitter/Periscope: @iamcarlajones
WEB: salonsolutionsgroup.com
EMAIL: carla@salonsolutionsgroup.com
LINKEDIN: www.linkedin.com/in/iamcarlajones

Angel Radcliffe, MBA is an Author, Public Speaker, Motivator and Entrepreneur with 10+ years' experience in the areas of Finance, Accounting & Technology. As the owner of CAS Consultants located in the Dallas-Fort Worth area, Ms. Radcliffe focuses on 'Empowering Entrepreneurs through Financial Management'. Ms. Radcliffe also provides services to small businesses relating to Financial Reporting, Analytics, & Real Estate Vendor Services.

A continued advocate of philanthropy, she currently serves on the Board of Directors for a local non-profit as Finance Chair and is dedicated to giving back to the community.

Ms. Radcliffe is a recipient of the 2016 National Financial Educators award. She aims to educate the community on Financial Literacy – Credit & Budget Management for consumers & small businesses.

You may connect with **Angel** below:

FACEBOOK: facebook.com/MissRMBA
FACEBOOK GROUP: facebook.com/groups/MSuite
IG/Twitter/Periscope: @MissRMBA
WEB: www.cas-consult.net
EMAIL: ARadcliffe@cas-consult.net

Chapter 1
Legitimizing Your Business

Legitimizing Your Business

Legitimizing your business is crucial to your success. In fact, many of these steps, if not all, can make or break you in your new venture. When missed, they can be detrimental to your business success and if implemented, can help you sleep well at night as a business owner.

Imagine, you have run a successful beauty salon for the past 15 years. Suddenly, you must uproot and move to a new state and you cannot take your clients with you. What do you do? You sell it, right? Well, what if you have never officially made it a business? What if you never registered the business name, established a business entity, or even opened a bank account? Suddenly, there is someone interested in purchasing the business, but they need a loan to do so. However, they cannot prove to the banks that the business is legitimate. These types of problems occur every day, because people fail to legitimize their businesses. Thus, causing major stress and aggravation in the long run.

Below you will find 5 *Steps to Legitimizing Your Business* and making sure it is legal and sellable should you ever desire to do so. The five steps are not finite or in any certain order. They are just some of the basic first steps that any entrepreneur needs to be take when initially launching the business and making certain that it remains both sustainable and profitable.

Legitimizing Your Business

Step #1 – *Check Your Company's Name*

The first step is to develop a business name. Then verify the availability of the name through your city and state and register it with both entities as well. Below is a scenario of a hair salon; Mary's Beauty Palace. The name is simple and Mary has driven all around the city and has not found one salon with that name. She has even checked her local business directory and has come up empty handed. She starts using the name without hesitation, but most importantly, without checking with her city and state to see if it is available *and* without registering it for herself.

One day Mary Johnson decides she wants to open a beauty salon in the same city, under the same name. She does a name search with the city and state and finds that the name is

Legitimizing Your Business

available. She then commences to register the name as well. A few more years pass and one day the first Mary decides to make her business "official". She lists her business in a few local online business directories and decides to finally register the name as well, until she discovers that Mary Johnson has already claimed it.

The first Mary is disappointed, because Mary Johnson legitimized her business first by registering the name properly; even though the first Mary had been in business longer. Unfortunately, the first Mary was never "officially" in business. She was simply doing hair from her basement. Now, when customers search for her, they get confused because they always end up talking to the wrong person on the phone. Or worst, they end up *in* the wrong salon. The moral of the story, conduct a name search and register your business with the appropriate city, state, and county offices immediately. Choosing and registering your business name is a key step to legally operating your business and possibly obtaining funding from the government.

- Domain Name – Not only do you want to register your business name, but you can also make sure that your domain name is available before you finalize your business name. If your domain name is not available with a .com extension, then a .net or a .co extension is perfectly fine. Think Nike, Dell, Apple, and even Google. People expect for your company's domain to be the same as your business name. If you cannot find one of the extensions mentioned, then consider other extensions released in 2015 such as; dot today, dot coach, dot guru, dot solutions, dot tech and so many more.

Legitimizing Your Business

Is your domain name the same as your business name? If not, do your customers have trouble finding you online? If so, you may want to get a new domain name with a different extension and forward your old name to your new name, so that those who are still using the old name will be able to find you.

Step #2 – *Get Insured*

One of the most crucial decisions many well intended business owners fail to make is obtain business insurance. The decision may be based on two reasons. First, they do not know they need it or they do not have the funds in the budget to obtain it. Not having business insurance can literally bankrupt your company and leave you and your family in a situation that makes you totally vulnerable to those who make it a habit of suing people for the heck of it.

So, what type of insurances are available to small business owners? Below are seven types of insurances that business owners should consider when opening a business based on their business needs.

1. **Worker's Compensation Insurance**
   Worker compensation laws vary from state to state. The state you're in determines how many employees you can have before you're required to carry this insurance. If your business meets the state requirements for the number of employees hired, you must add it to your business insurance policy to cover accidents, disability, and deaths that are a result of the job. For example, after 4 employees, you must carry this insurance in the state of Alabama.

Legitimizing Your Business

2. **Property Insurance**
   Whether a business owns or leases its facilities, property insurance is needed to protect the overall business, including signage, equipment loss or damage, fire, and theft. Natural catastrophes such as floods, tornadoes, and earthquakes are usually not covered or require different types of coverage. Therefore, you should check with your agent to make sure you have the right types of coverage and coverage combinations.

3. **Professional Liability Insurance**
   Also, known as errors and omissions insurance, professional liability insurance covers businesses against harmful claims of negligence due to mistakes or a failure to perform. Insurance agents, realtors, and notaries typically must carry this type of coverage.

4. **Homeowner's or Renter's Insurance**
   If you work from home, your homeowner's policy will not cover your business, but in most cases, you can speak with your provider to have your equipment and supplies covered under additional insurance.

5. **Vehicle Insurance**
   If company vehicles are being used, they should be fully covered to protect your business against liability claims in the event of an accident.

Legitimizing Your Business

6. **Product Liability Insurance**
   If your company manufactures products for the general marketplace, you want to make sure, to obtain this insurance to protect your business from claims made because of products sold causing harm to a consumer. Even if you think your product is completely safe, the truth is, you can never be too safe when in business. Product liability insurance can be tailored to your specific product.

7. **Business Interruption Insurance**
   Depending on your type of business, a disaster or catastrophic event can cause a business' doors to shut down temporarily and lose substantial income. If your business requires a physical space to conduct business, such as a retail space, this type of insurance is mandatory.

Were there insurances mentioned here that you had not considered for your business? Which insurances do you still need?

Legitimizing Your Business

Step #3 – *Get a Logo*

A logo helps to establish the business/business owner as a professional. It also helps to create brand loyalty and brand recognition. Children often learn to recognize logos before they even learn to read. Think of McDonald's and those big golden arches. For one, they place them so high on the outside of their retail stores, they can be seen a mile away. Children and adults alike recognize those arches. McDonalds has done such a great job creating brand awareness all over the world. Like those arches, logos help assist businesses in standing out from the competition through brand recognition. When you effectively market your business through your logo like Jordan sneakers, Apple computers, and Mercedes, people do not soon forget your brand.

Versatility is the key. The logo needs to be versatile enough to be placed on t-shirts, pens, folders, notepads, and everything else in between. When designing a logo, you should consider the color, what the image means, if the logo aligns with the business name, and if the logo can to be reduced small enough to be used on ink pens, pendants, and more. Remember though, less is more. Keep your logo simple, think Apple.

Do you have a logo? Do people recognize it when they see it? Is it scaled properly? Meaning, does it look the same on a t-shirt as it does on an ink pen? What makes good logos stand out to you? Did you know that popular brands like Starbucks are always changing their brand image and updating their logos? To stay fresh and current, it is imperative to keep your logo fresh by making minor edits to it periodically.

Legitimizing Your Business

Step #4 – Establish a Strong Foundation for Your Brand

There are many components of branding including but not limited to, customer service, colors of the business logo, the company slogan and business cards. Some established and new business owners do not understand the meaning of creating a brand or various components that go into building a brand. So, what is branding? Well, in a nutshell, branding is everything. Branding ranges from the way a team answers the phones, to the colors of your logo, on down to a company's slogans and business cards. Almost any and everything a business can imagine, is connected to a company's brand.

Creating a well-designed logo is imperative from the beginning. Consider best practices when designing the logo. It is important to have marketing material created that align with branding representation. For instance, brochures, business cards, and the company's website should be free of typos and updated frequently. All branding material should have the same color scheme, logos, and slogans. Consistency is key to creating a brand that customers remember and identify to link them to the business.

Do you have a strong brand? Do people recognize your company when they see your logo or hear your slogan or tagline? Companies brand and rebrand themselves all the time. Be sure to constantly improve the business and branding as needed.

Legitimizing Your Business

Step #5 – *Build a Place Online to do Business with Your Customers*

There used to be a time when businesses were discovered using the Yellow Pages and if someone wanted to ask a question or get information, they would call the company and/or waited for them to send an information packet in the mail. Back then, everyone was not in the business directory and they were not expected to be. Most people conducted business locally and by word of mouth. However, the Internet began to change all of that. Today, almost any question you want answered can be found on a company's website. No one expects you NOT to have a website and if a potential customer or client cannot find the business on the Internet, they almost assume the business does not exist.

Legitimizing Your Business

The bottom line is, doing business in today's marketplace without a website and social media, is like doing business without a telephone number or email address. Simply put, a website provides a global online presence for customers to do business with any company.

Are you aware of how much money you could possibly be leaving on the table by not having a web presence and not having testimonials from your customers and clients? Remember, people do business with those who they know, like, and trust. Web presence allows potential customers to get to know the business and learn to trust its legitimacy.

Chapter 2
Building Business Credit

Building Business Credit

Credit is essential for any growing business. Business credit allows you to reserve your profits in exchange for a line of credit or a loan. As an entrepreneur, credit is pertinent to your growth and you should do your research to find out the steps to take in order to build your credit up.

So, why does a business need credit anyway? Well, let's say business is going great, but once you look at the numbers, you are just at the break-even point. You suddenly have an influx of orders for products and you do not have the capital to put those items in production. Or, let's say for instance, you are receiving more business than you can handle. You may want to consider hiring staff or you may need to order supplies. This is where business credit comes in handy. Business credit allows you to have additional monies available to you aside from your revenue and as you make timely payments, your business becomes more creditworthy.

One of the reasons many businesses fail or completely become defunct is due to lack of revenue or financial sources. If your business is at a point where you no longer have the means to order supplies, pay employees, or act on orders, business credit may work for you. Many entrepreneurs may be at a standstill because they simply do not know how to build business credit.

Let's look at the *5 Steps* toward helping you build business credit. With these *5 Steps*, you will be equipped with the knowledge to build it and potentially grow your business.

Building Business Credit

Step #1 - *Incorporate Your Business*

Before attempting to build business credit, your business should be 'legitimized.' Legitimizing means obtaining an EIN number and being incorporated. Incorporating your business allows you to protect your personal assets from additional taxes and legal claims. However, what most people do not know is that business credit cannot be built as a sole proprietor.

If you have not yet incorporated your business and are still operating as a sole proprietor, the first step is to incorporate. To do so, you need to contact the IRS and complete the paperwork to obtain a new EIN number. These steps can quickly be executed on their website at www.irs.gov.

Building Business Credit

Once you have completed the proper paperwork to incorporate your business, you then need to file the articles of incorporation with the state you plan on starting your business in. The fees for filing your articles of incorporation vary from state to state. You will need to research those costs and procedures with your local Secretary of State office. Also, if your business will be charging sales tax, you will need to register with your state comptroller's office for a sales and use tax permit.

Are you unsure of which business structure to choose?
Research, research, and research! Check out the options for types of corporations versus an LLC versus a non-profit, etc., and how each one would fit your business. Be sure to look at the tax options and fees associated with each structure, as well as how taxes play a role in business structures overall.

Building Business Credit

Step # 2 - *Open a Business Bank Account*

Once your business is legitimized, you now have the ability to open a business bank account. A business bank account is necessary to separate personal expenses from business expenses. You should never co-mingle your personal income and expenses with your business revenue and expenses. To open a business bank account, you need to complete the process of legitimizing your business. Remember, you cannot open a business bank account without an EIN number.

If you have chosen to incorporate your business, you will also need your official filings/articles of incorporation to present to the bank. Make certain to shop around and compare banking options that best fit you and your business. Some things to look out for are monthly fees, deposit minimums, transaction

Building Business Credit

costs, bank reputation, branch locations, and benefits to small business owners. There are some banks who offer products for new entrepreneurs. Look very closely at bank account options with the future of your business in mind.

Do you already have a business bank account? If so, would you like to change banks? *There is nothing wrong with opening a new account if you are dissatisfied with your current banking. Just be sure to keep records from your old account for bookkeeping and tax purposes.*

Step #3 - *Obtain a DUNS Number (Dun & Bradstreet)*

A DUNS number is a nine-digit identifier, similar to an EIN, used to build a credit profile with Dun & Bradstreet. Dun & Bradstreet is a commercial company providing data related to credit history sales marketing and risk with businesses. Obtaining a DUNS number is a simple process and is free of charge to small business owners. A DUNS number is used in addition to the EIN number when applying for business credit and accounts with suppliers & vendors. Having a DUNS number makes your business more credible with lenders and customers as they can verify public financial data. It also allows you to do business overseas and obtain government contracts. Applications for a DUNS number can be completed online at www.dandb.com.

When applying for your number you will need to provide information regarding your business such as:

- Legal Business Name
- DBA - If Applicable
- Business Address
- Business Phone Number
- Business Structure

Building Business Credit

- Number of Employees
- Contact Name & Title of the Person Applying

The application process for a DUNS number can take up to 30 days or you can expedite the process and have your number within 5 days using 'DUNSFile' via the Dun & Bradstreet website at www.dandb.com.

Building Business Credit

Can anyone apply for a DUNS number? How would customers/creditors or potential partners know if I have a DUNS number?

Yes, any business is eligible to apply for a DUNS number.

On the Dun & Bradstreet website www.dnb.com there is a 'DUNS lookup' by company name and location.

Step # 4 - *Open Accounts with Vendors & Suppliers*

Vendor and/or supplier accounts are a sure way to get your business credit profile started.

Building Business Credit

Check with your lender or supplier to see if net 30/45 accounts are offered and reported to the credit bureaus and/or Dun & Bradstreet. Typically, it's easier to open a vendor/supplier account versus a major credit card for your business. There are suppliers who will work with small business owners in obtaining business credit. You may want to start with small orders to build up a good payment history and consistency.

An example would be ordering ink cartridges or inexpensive office supplies. Within 30 days or 45 days, depending on your agreement, you would make a small payment or pay that balance in full. Keep track of your business credit profiles on Experian, TransUnion, Equifax and Dun & Bradstreet. As a result, you should see your business credit score rising with timely payments of your supplier & vendor accounts. Once you have a history of six or more months of timely payments, you may qualify for an unsecured small business credit card.

What is needed to apply for a vendor/supplier credit account? What are some examples of vendors/suppliers offering this benefit?

To apply for a vendor/supplier credit account you will need to supply pertinent information in regards to your business. Information requested can be general business name, DBA owner information, business partner information, address, phone number, business banking information, as well as your business banker's contact phone number. You may also be asked for other credit references from other supplier vendor accounts. Examples of vendors or suppliers offering credit accounts are: Staples, Office Depot, Quill, Newegg and Uline. Again, be sure to do your research on whichever

Building Business Credit

company you're ordering from to see if they offer a net 30 or net 45 credit account for small business owners.

Step #5 - *Obtain a Secure Credit Card or Line of Credit*

Obtaining a secured credit card or a secured line of credit is another way to get your business credit going. Unsecured business credit cards or a secured business line of credit works the same as a personal secured account. With secure accounts, you provide money upfront and the bank or lender either grants you a credit card for that same amount or a line of credit for that same amount. You would then make timely payments for six to 12 months with hopes of the bank turning the account into an unsecured credit card or line of credit.

Building Business Credit

There are many banks and credit unions that offer secured business credit cards or secured lines of credit. A recommendation would be to check with your bank where you hold a small business account to see if this is something which is offered. Compare various options to see which bank works best with small business owners. Just as with any account, when trying to build business credit you want to be sure that the account data will be reported to the major credit bureaus and possibly Dun & Bradstreet.

How much is needed to open a secured business card or secured line of credit?

Depending on the bank or credit union you can open a secured business credit card or start a secured line of credit with a minimum of $500.

Chapter 3
Apps You Need In Business

Apps You Need In Business

FINANCIAL MANAGEMENT

Poor Financial Management is one of the top reasons small businesses fail, per the Small Business Administration. Many businesses lack financial management and proper record keeping. However, technology has made it easier to manage financial records as a small business owner. Listed below are two apps which have become a necessity an as entrepreneur to keep up with your revenues & expenses.

Expensify – Technology has allowed us to remove the daunting task of shuffling through financial paperwork. Expensify is an awesome app that links to your bank account to pull in transactional data and is available on IOS/Android, & also has web login capability. Allowing you to view and manage your company's expenses; you can run an expense report with the push of a button from your phone, compile reports, and email directly from the app.

Smart Receipts – If you are tired of holding onto, or losing paper receipts, this app is for you. Smart Receipts allows you to take a picture of your receipts; the application reads and records them, ridding the need for manual input. It also allows expense tracking on the go, you can download a report by month or week and email to yourself or your accountant. Smart Receipts serves as an awesome backup for those who have trouble keeping up with paper receipts.

Apps You Need In Business

MILEAGE

One of the top missed tax deductions for small business owners is mileage. Many small businesses are failing to keep track of mileage and vehicle expenses, not realizing that mileage can be a huge benefit when filing taxes. Small businesses in particular need to know how many miles and exactly which vehicle expenses can be claimed.

Mile IQ - Available on both Android & IOS, once you download the app to your phone or tablet, it runs in the background. Mile IQ picks up movement and categorizes all movement into 'drives'. At the end of each day, you can re-categorize the drives into a 'personal' or 'business' category. The app also tracks mileage and expenses such as parking and tolls with an "in app" expense tracker. A tax feature included, is the IRS mileage rate, which is also auto calculated and updated each year with rate changes within the app. As a result, at the end of the year, you will already have your mileage totaled and categorized, making it easier to decide on a standard versus actual tax deduction for your business. Mile IQ is also available for full access on the web for data and reporting needs; you can run a daily, weekly, or monthly report from the web or app to view expenses for each vehicle.

CONTACT MANAGEMENT

As a small business owner, you are meeting new people all the time; from networking events to conferences. It's common to lose a business card or two along the way, but if you are tired

Apps You Need In Business

of losing them or worst yet, having to manually input contacts into your phone or database system, you should consider a contact management application.

CamCard – CamCard is your electronic rolodex, available on Android & IOS, it allows you to electronically store your business card and send to others. This app also allows users to take pictures of business cards you receive and have the information stored electronically, therefore allowing a digital copy of the person's information instantly. However, one of the best benefits of this app is that each time you add new contacts to the CamCard database, you can transport the email address to your mailing list.

CONTENT MANAGEMENT

Content management is also key to staying organized in business. Keeping track of your next tasks or remembering the idea you had over coffee can be taxing on the brain. A great content management system can help you remember and store every great idea and conversation in one easy to manage location.

Evernote – Evernote is an app that allows every idea to be remembered, shared, and collaborated on. Entrepreneurs often have the next great idea percolating in their brain, but they may not be in a place to put it on paper. Evernote allows the user to take notes/tasks and share them with others or email them to yourself. The app is also useful if you are

Apps You Need In Business

collaborating on ideas with others; the sharing allows for instant feedback.

These are the top 5 recommended apps for small business owners. Challenge yourself to download them all and try them if you are not using them already, you will not be disappointed. Technology is forever changing and as a small business owner you must keep up with anything beneficial to your businesses' efficiency and success and that's exactly what these apps are designed for.

What applications are you currently using for business? Could any of the above-mentioned apps help increase efficiency in your business?

Chapter 4
Building a Badass Brand

Building a Badass Brand

If there is an open question of which came first the chicken or the egg, I certainly believe that same school of thought exist in relation to branding and marketing. As a new business owner or someone who is contemplating a journey into business ownership, it is a necessary exercise to understand what a brand is and how you well determine, design, and communicate your brand and its message to your targeted consumer or customer.

An often-initial mistake made by new business owners is to begin marketing activities before one has completed a thorough brand assessment for their business and its product(s).

To begin, let's get a clearer understanding of a brand and identify the five steps to consider when building a recognizable and respected badass brand.

A simple definition of a brand is promises made by a business or person about a business and or a personal brand that consumers or clients believe in. In short, it articulates through messaging and visual, what the business will be known for. Branding answers the questions: who you are, what benefits your business or services will offer or satisfy? Branding is something that through experience remains consistent and happens at every consumer or customer touch point along the customer journey.

Building a Badass Brand

A brand consists of the following:

- Brand Attributes - Characteristics that identify the brand visually, verbally and behaviorally.
- Brand Equity - The economic value placed on a brand and its assets.
- Brand Identity - The look and feel. (Logos, fonts, colors, photos, design, etc.)
- Brand Image - How one perceives, feels, or believes about the brand.
- Positioning Statement - The statement that captures the essence of the brand.
- Brand Promise - What the brand says it will deliver and the consumer can expect.

However, understanding brand components is the easiest part of the branding exercise. Determining how to brand your business or personal brand is the elephant in the room and the true challenge of the business concerning their customer and their products and or services. Below are 5 *steps* that will get you started and well on your way to building a Badass brand.

Building a Badass Brand

Step #1 - *Defining Your Audience*

Often time this is an area that is much easier to discuss than to determine. However, let's look at some simple ways to define your audience.

- Who are the people who are willing or currently paying for your product and or service?
- Who are the people that are currently influencing others to purchase your product or service?
- Who are your loyal advocates or ambassadors for your business, its products and services?

Building a Badass Brand

Keeping the above three things at "top of mind", let's take this one step further and now breathe life into who your ideal customer is by:

- Giving them a name (John, Mark, Marissa, Barbara, etc.)
- Defining their lifestyle (healthy, lavish, modest, minimalist, etc.)
- Defining their behaviors and interest (timely, bicycle riding, reading, etc.)
- Defining their gender
- Defining their education status/level, income

Take a moment to consider who your ideal audience may be. Now that you have thought about your ideal audience, are you currently servicing your ideal audience member/members?

Building a Badass Brand

Step #2 - *Deciding What You Will Sacrifice to Own*

When brand focused, you must be willing to center your attention on that very thing you want to be known for. Also, consider how you will communicate that very message to your ideal customer and or client. As a licensed industry professional who also has over 30 years as a senior corporate leader, I could have very well selected as my ideal customer, small business owners from any industry that were looking for business development, coaching, and consulting. However, I chose not to be a generalist in the coaching and consulting business arena but to *own* coaching and consulting for the health and beauty industry professional.

Building a Badass Brand

Giving time to determine what it is that you and your business are willing to sacrifice to own, will help guide what is required to build a badass brand and one that stands out in your chosen market and with your chosen customers or consumers.

What do you see as the competitive space your brand can own?

Building a Badass Brand

Step #3 – *It Really Is All About Your Core User*

In step one of this chapter we discussed elements that help identify your audience. In this step, we will drill down and discuss the core user within your total audience. We are not talking about the person who has heard of your brand and mentioned it as an alternative to something else. On the contrary, we are talking about that person or group of persons who directly help drive purchase intent for your business product and or service. They are those that choose your product and or its services first above all others. They are not willing to substitute. They believe in your company's core values and embrace and identify with how those core values

Building a Badass Brand

are exemplified through all facets of your business and how they experience it.

The core user IS your LOYAL BUSINESS ADVOCATE. They are not price sensitive or price driven when it comes to your product or service. They have a distinct buyer behavior that resonates with your product, its message, benefits, and features. A core user can be identified and defined as discussed when determining your audience. You see, your audience are those in the brand cycle. The core user again is the one that defines your brand.

Defining the core user is critical to any brand. Without clarity in relation to core user(s), there is no sustainable growth, business success or longevity.

Who do you think your CORE USER is?

Building a Badass Brand

Step #4 - *Frame of Reference*

When your prospective customer or consumer thinks of your brand, its product or service, what category do they think about? Understanding or determining this is known as the "frame of reference". When I think of Frito Lay, I think of potato chips/snacks. I don't think of chocolate. On the other hand, if I think of Godiva', I do think about chocolate.

Allowing a customer or consumer to have the wrong frame of reference for your business product and/or services could be detrimental to your business and your brand. Being able to make it clear as to what your business does and who the

Building a Badass Brand

business does it for, helps the user to put your brand in the correct "Frame of Reference."

Here are three things the "Frame of Reference" should do for your brand.

- Support the brand positioning;
- Choose a competitive "frame of reference" that narrows the number of brands that would be competing in that space, and,
- Connects your benefits to the consumer/core user by establishing it in its most positive light.

What do you think is your brand's "Frame of Reference" ?

Building a Badass Brand

Step #5 - *Brand Benefits*

Lastly, our discussion centers on the brand's benefits. The brand benefits are all the things the brand delivers back to the core user.

In branding activities with current and future clients, focus is directed on efforts of branding that appeals to three areas.

- **Feelings**- What emotional cord are you trying to touch with your brand? What satisfaction does the brand provide to the core user?
- **Intra-Personal** – Intra-personal answers the "what's in it for me (WIIFM) statement or question." Core users typically want to know how the brand can or will satisfy their need when they experience the brand.

Building a Badass Brand

Again, does it satisfy them rationally and intrapersonally?
- **Need Resolution** - What can the brand do for the core user? The brand must be able to deliver as consistency is always key. Again, brand promises must be fulfilled each time the core user experiences the brand.

In the end, building a badass brand is not just about doing or delivering your promise and brand experience sometimes. Badass brands are just that because they deliver each time for the core user. They don't just meet the core user needs periodically but are known because they consistently exceed the core user's needs, desires, and expectations.

What would your current core user describe as your brand benefits?

Chapter 5
Sealing the Deal with Clients

Sealing the Deal with Clients

You have a business. Now what? You have a product or service. Now what? The next question is not "do you have a customer", but more importantly do you have the right customer who is interested in what you have to offer or sell? Two of the most important factors to consider when building your clientele, consumer or customer base for your business is customer acquisition and building sustainable, long-term customer relationships. As a current or future business owner, understanding who you will serve is critical to developing the right strategy that will determine how you will serve your ideal client.

In this chapter, we place emphasis on client relationship(s). Provide a roadmap to successful positioning, customer identification/acquisition, building trust, effective messaging and customer satisfaction. Understanding the role and relationship of each client relationship will make it clearer which to choose that can solidify and seal the deal with your clients.

Sealing the Deal with Clients

Step #1 – *POSITIONING: How, Who and Why*

Positioning is all about strategy and how one or an organization employs those strategies to achieve desired business goals and or objectives. Positioning is a way the business can reach an ideal customer, client or core user. For an organization to maximize its positioning strategy, the business must identify the following:

- Who the customer is and what the business wants to be known for in their current market and to the customers they currently or desire to serve.
- Assess current strengths, weaknesses, opportunities and threats both internally and externally. This

Sealing the Deal with Clients

   identifies the current market, current market competitors and the businesses desired customer.
- How it will the business differentiate itself in the market place. Differentiation is not just about the product or service. It also provides identifiable, competitive points of difference. It answers the question for the customer, client or core user as to what is unique, different or better about your business, its product and or service(s).

Positioning matters. Positioning is the guiding force behind your brand. Positioning allows you to communicate and connect. It will never be about 'what' in relation to positioning; it will always be about 'how'.

What position does your business hold in the mind of your customer, client or core user and how can you leverage your current position in your current market for business success?

Sealing the Deal with Clients

Step #2 – *Client Acquisition*

Once you have determined how you will be positioned in your current marketplace, it's time to look at what is necessary when it comes to acquiring a client. Some may have heard or even use the term, "client acquisition". Client acquisition as defined by businessdictionary.com, is "The process of persuading a consumer to purchase a company's goods or services". The cost associated with the important customer acquisition process is an important measure for a business to evaluate in combination with how much value having each customer typically brings to the business.

When we think or speak about client acquisition, one might think about the cost to acquire a client versus client

Sealing the Deal with Clients

acquisition as it relates to targeting the right customer for your business. Giving consideration to identifying who the business will serve, defining the target market is the first step in the road to client acquisition. If you don't know who you will serve, you will never know what is required to gain a future client either in cost or action. Here are a few things to consider when defining your target market or as they are often referred to as your ideal client avatar (ICA), client demographics or client archetype.

For me the easiest way to define this is to create a client persona based on:

- What product or service to be offered;
- The problem the service or product solves and;
- What client type or persona would benefit most by using the product and or service offering?

Consideration must also be given to the customer's, client and or core user interest, behaviors, gender, age, education and income among other things. These factors help determine your target market. Once these have been identified, now identify the best way to attract and/or acquire this client.

What activities have you identified that are necessary to attract your ideal client and what strategies will you employ to acquire them?

Sealing the Deal with Clients

Step #3 – *Building Customer Trust*

Earlier in the chapter, it was mentioned that a critical component to sealing the deal with your client is to build long-term sustainable relationships. Achieving this in today's business arena has never been easier now with the ability to communicate and connect at literally the push of a button or a simple social media post. Regardless of the medium used to reach a client, building trust is critical. We now speak in terms of authenticity, the "know, like and trust" factor and how doing so now is the key both on and offline. However, the foundation that supports all that rests in the ability to articulate a level of competency, expertise or thought leadership.

If you have any experience with customer acquisition directly or indirectly, you will more than likely have recognized that consumers are more demanding and more savvy. The reason we have identified is the access through internet, social media and live streaming. This has caused the playing field for

Sealing the Deal with Clients

businesses products and services to play in a more congested arena than ever before. Businesses no longer can make the mistake of getting any part of the customer journey or experience wrong. Why? There are just too many options available for customers to choose from now.

Credibility is the secret to building customer relationships and trust. Being consistently present along with delivering value every time aids in closing the gap and sealing the deal with customer trust.

What have you done to gain customer trust and what impact has this had in your business?

Sealing the Deal with Clients

Step #4 – *Communication or Messaging*

It is about both communication and messaging. We often say to clients, "It's not what you say, but rather how you say it." Customers now want businesses that are present. Customers also have higher expectations from businesses they choose to do business with. Messaging and communication is all about connecting. Connecting requires that one masters positioning, identification of their target market to acquire their ideal customer and build customer trust and credibility. Messaging and communication is also about how the business can articulate its value.

Messaging tells the appropriate story of the company, its brand, product and service. It also clarifies what problem it solves, how it solves them and the benefit to the customer. If a

Sealing the Deal with Clients

business cannot communicate the message in the manner that resonates with their ideal client, the individual, company or organization won't exist for long. To ensure messaging is aligned with the customer and their needs, create a tool that can be used to gauge effectiveness and customer response. One way would be to survey your current and/or prospective customer(s).

What have you found to be the most effective way to deliver your business message to your customer, client or core user?

Sealing the Deal with Clients

Step #5 – *Customer Satisfaction: It Really Does Matter*

Business is about creating an experience, providing a service or product in a manner that doesn't just meet the customer's expectation, but exceeds the expectation. While organizations list customer satisfaction often as one of its core values, most don't give it focus or priority. Customer satisfaction is not something that just happens. Companies that have excelled at the delivery of customer satisfaction may often find that having systems and consistent procedures in place, provide for delivery excellence and standardization of the delivery process. Customer satisfaction and care also requires resources to support its ongoing practice and delivery

Sealing the Deal with Clients

throughout every aspect of the business, its products and services.

A few sound practices that can be activated within an organization to ensure the highest level of customer satisfaction and/or care are to:

- Begin with an integrated "customer care" plan. This plan is based on a 360 approach of implementation, tracking, evaluating, modifying, communicating, etc.
- Develop an internal system for consistent communication and training in how the product or service should be delivered, the environment in which it is to happen and how each level within the customer care plan is to be measured and tracked.
- Every individual should have a role and be held accountable.
- The business must have a way for the customer to communicate their experience.
- The business must be prepared to react with a sense of urgency that again is communicated to the user of their products and/or services.

A business can never be comfortable with either their performance, nor with how their customers' experience the environment in which their products and/or services are purchased or used. Keep in mind customers not only speak with their physical or social voices, but they also speak with their dollars. One of your main goals is that they continue or begin to spend their dollars in your business.

Sealing the Deal with Clients

What is your current level of customer satisfaction? How do you measure and how often is it measured for your company or organization?

Chapter 6
Collaborating with Any Team

Collaborating with Any Team

In the beginning, being an entrepreneur can mean wearing multiple hats. You might think having a partner would make your life and your business run a whole lot smoother. Although that can be true in a lot of ways, having a partner can also add another level of complication to how you do business. Being in partnership with others can be both rewarding and taxing if not executed properly. Partnering with others has its pros and cons. This should be carried forth with a great deal of caution and pre-planning.

Here are 5 *steps* to help you get started on the right track when working with any team. These precautions will not only protect your business, but they can also protect the relationship between you and your new partner(s), because typically when we think of partnering with others, it is usually someone we already have close ties to, like a family member or a friend. However, these relationships can be damaged permanently if the business goes south and businesses, as well as relationships, usually go south when proper planning is not done on the front end.

Collaborating with Any Team

Step 1 - *The Partner(s) Must Have Common Objectives*

Every team should have one goal; to focus on the objectives of the project. When starting, any new venture involving a team, it is crucial that the group agrees on the objectives of the project or business venture at the beginning. For example, if you start a real estate firm with your best friend from college and *your* objective is to build upscale condos for millennials who want to live just outside of the city, but your business partners' objective is to build high rise apartments for seniors, then there is a conflict and you probably should not consider moving forward until you are both on the same page. The key is to make certain that you and your business partner(s) see eye to eye from the beginning. Otherwise, projects can be delayed, friendships can be ruined, and monies can be lost, amongst other things.

Collaborating with Any Team

The best way to make certain the goals and objectives are met for the project is to lay everything out on the table. Here are a few tips to help you get started.

- Have each person to identify why they want to pursue said project. Is it to fill a need, make money, create opportunities, or something else. These questions can be addressed in a simple conversation with the entire team and will let people know if this venture is worth pursuing for them.

- Create a contract agreement to make everything official. It should include a timeframe for reaching your goals and objectives, what happens if they aren't reached on time, how to deal with disputes, money, and everything else worth mentioning. All parties should sign this at the beginning.

- Layout an exit strategy. This strategy will outline how the partners are to sell the business, relinquish their rights to the business, or walk away if things seemly aren't going well. This is a step that most do not think about until they are forced to do so.

- Decided how monies will be split and disbursed between members. Determine who will own certain percentages of the business. (This should also be put into the contract) Will you have joint or separate accounts? Will the business revenue be split straight down the middle or in portions, with a portion going back to the business and the remainder being split between the partners?

Collaborating with Any Team

Do not ignore the above tips and pay a great deal of attention to the details when putting together the bylaws (which will be discussed later) and when creating any type of agreements between the partners. As mentioned before, these tips and steps are mentioned to help you save time, money, and confusion down the road. Granted, not every recommendation will work for every situation. Read each step carefully to decide which is right for your project or business. Proceed with care and caution. Doing things right from the start is the key to long term success.

Step 2 – *Learn the Art of Working with Any Teams Skillsets*

Ever been on a team where the members had similar skillsets and continuously stepped on each other's toes because everyone wanted to do the other persons' job? Or, a situation where a skillset was missing and thus, work couldn't get done? Worse yet, no one knew who was good at what and there was no order to how things got done. A great team is created when each member brings something unique to the table and people respect each persons' contribution. If each person focuses on doing what they are good at and what they have been assigned to do, the project runs smoothly and is completed on schedule and with minimal conflict, but if they do not, projects could go on forever; wasting a lot of time and money along the way.

Problems can arise when working with teams where there is no structure and no real leadership. To work effectively, two things need to occur. First, the skillsets of the team members need to be accessed for the task. Determine which skills are needed and which are present amongst your group and then assign individual task per your findings. Two, outline the

Collaborating with Any Team

scope of work to be done from the beginning to the end and assign someone like a "Task Keeper" to make sure everyone stays on schedule and focused specifically on their task only.

You will be amazed at the results you get when you employ this simple method for getting things done *and* people will be more willing to answer to one person whose job is to keep everyone on track, than to answer to the entire team, unless it is necessary of course. Using these steps and simple methods are easy to follow and only require a little planning on the front end. Remember, each person comes to the table with a different set of skills. Allowing people to work within their strengths will guarantee you get better results out of them and having people to respect boundaries and not do the jobs of others will make everyone feel respected, as well as successful, as they carry out their said roles. Delegating this way should assure that work is done to a higher standard than if people were working in areas they were not confident or comfortable in. The overall goal is to successfully get the job done.

Step 3 *- Create a Non-Disclosure Agreement*

Non-Disclosure Agreements or NDA's as they are known, are designed to protect business ideas that are sensitive in nature. Unique designs, special engineering, patents, and anything one can think of that has not been brought to the market and could be stolen by someone else if shared is just one reason to make a potential partner or investor sign an NDA before sharing your idea with them.

A company can either print one off the Internet or have their attorney draw one up for them. If the company can afford it, having an attorney to draft it up is ideal. An attorney will

Collaborating with Any Team

consider loop holes and clauses that the business owner may have never even thought of. This simple step can mean the difference between a business being legally protected and having a leg to stand on should they ever need to sue someone in a court of law for stealing their idea and *not* being able to prove that they ever shared their idea at all or if they shared it, not being able to prove whose idea it was from the beginning. *NDA's* are popular in many business ventures that involve unique ideas, but they are extremely popular in the technical world. Though these agreements are common in the tech world, usually they are meant for collaborators, as investors tend to balk at such agreements. Here are a few reasons why a company might need to consider creating an NDA.

1. A potential partner shifts the conversation from "what" the project involves to "how" the company plans to get it done. This could lead to trade secrets or highly secretive information being shared and stolen. An NDA will prevent sharing sensitive data or documents with a third party that you do not want extrapolated in any way.
2. A company is having talks with a possible collaborator who is not necessarily an investor and one who stands to benefit greatly from the collaboration if they decide to do it themselves.
3. The company has invested a ton of money and time in the venture and they do not want someone to run off with their ideas.
4. NDA's prevent or lessen the possibility of having to take someone to court, because of them stealing, copying, or sharing confidential information.

Collaborating with Any Team

Each reason points out the importance of NDA's and its benefits. Hiring an attorney to draft the NDA for new business owners is recommended. Remember, to consider budgeting throughout the entire process. If the plan is to place a lot of money into the project or if a lot of money has already been spent, then it is a good idea to invest the money to hire an attorney to protect the company's unique idea from current and future threats.

Step 4 - *Create a Contract*

Having an attorney to draft a contract agreement could be a very wise investment. If the company can't afford to hire an attorney and decides to draft the document themselves, it is a great idea to have the attorney review the document before using it. A good attorney will likely see things that others

Collaborating with Any Team

probably will not catch based on their level of knowledge with contracts in general.

In the contract, layout how things will be handle if the business is a success and if it is not. Also, include how partners will exit the business should it reach a point of extinction or if it reaches a point where one partner wants to sell. Again, the whole idea is for the business to be a success and people sell successful businesses every day.

Step 5 - *Create Bylaws to Govern How Things Get Done*

Bylaws are a company's bible. They outline the roles within the organization, duties and responsibilities, when meetings are held, and how to settle disputes within the partnership. Depending on the size and function of the business or project, topics may be included or omitted as needed. Below is an outline of the sections that should be included in a set of business bylaws.

- **Name of the Organization** - Be as specific as possible about the name. Is the business incorporated? Is it a non-profit? Include any extensions to the name i.e. LLC, Inc., Co., etc. Remember, whatever is placed here, should be consistent in all other places.

- **Object or Purpose** - In one simple sentence, be clear and concise. Why does the business exist and what is it organized to do? If at any time the business owner changes course and decides to do something else, the objective should also change within the bylaws.

Collaborating with Any Team

- **Members** - Here you will include the member's names, whether there are dues to be paid and any additional responsibilities. You can also add classes of members here. For instance, what does it mean to be an active member vs. an inactive member. The bylaws should define what it takes for one to be an inactive member and what it takes for a member to be considered an inactive member. Additionally, this section includes eligibility for membership as well as the cost associated with dues and fees. Lastly, this section should also include disciplinary procedures and resignation expectations and requirements.

- **Officers** - List the officers within the organization, their specific duties, the procedures and process for nominating and electing officers, and how vacancies are addressed. The officers should be listed in order of ranking.

- **Meetings** - The articles will include which day of week meetings will take place and the frequency of the meetings. The meetings section discusses quorums and the terms of holding "special meetings" of attendance. Additionally, the meeting section outlines attendance expectations, including ramifications for absences.

Make certain to do your homework and research. Every set of bylaws are different, depending upon the business. There are several good examples to follow on the Internet which you can pull information from to establish a good set of bylaws for your new business venture.

Collaborating with Any Team

The *5 steps* mentioned are not the *only* ones to be taken to assure the team starts off in the right direction. There are several other steps to help the collaboration run smoothly, i.e., creating terms and conditions, establishing a possible project commitment letter, which can also include a process commitment agreement for the team. However, one of the most important thing any team can do is to make sure there is synergy for the vision of the business or project and there is room for flexibility.

Before beginning, the team needs to know and understand the purpose of coming together and creating the business entity in the first place. They should identify the decision maker. If it is the business owner, then the hard work has already been done. The point is, the decision maker can make certain things are not at a standstill due to too many chiefs and not enough Indians.

Having a decision maker may even seem unnecessary when people are simply trying to write a book together as an example, but when things are at a standstill and progress can't be made, only a mediator or decision maker can help things move along. This person can solve disputes, hold other members accountable and makes sure things run smoothly. They will refer to the contract and bylaws that govern "how things get done" and use that as their basis for good decision making.

In conclusion, bylaws assist with having accountability mechanisms in place. Accountability establishes agreed upon roles that each member of the team adheres to. As mentioned earlier, there should always be someone in place that makes

Collaborating with Any Team

certain things get done and people stay accountable; a decision maker or task master are ideal. Having these mechanisms in place before beginning can make or break your venture. As Benjamin Franklin once said, "when you fail to plan, you are planning to fail". The goal is to be successful and with that in mind, preparation comes first.

Appendix

Appendix

Appendix

Appendix

New Business Owner's Checklist

Checklist		Notes
☐	Decide on a Business Name	
☐	Decide on Business Structure	
☐	What is the Initial Investment?	
☐	Create A Business Plan	
☐	Apply for an EIN	
☐	Register Your Business with the City/State	
☐	Register DBA If Using a Different Name	
☐	Apply for a DUNS Number	
☐	Establish a Business Address (ex: P.O Box)	

Appendix

☐	Open a Business Bank Account	
☐	Establish a Business Website	
☐	Order Business Cards	
☐	Attend Training/Workshops	
☐	Join Networking Groups	
☐	Retain a Small Business Mentor/Coach	
☐	Order Marketing Materials	
☐	Apply for Business Credit	
☐	Choose a Financial Software	
☐	Apply for Business Licenses (Sales/Use Tax) etc.	
☐	Obtain Small Business Insurance	
☐	Rent Office Space If Needed	

Appendix

☐	Create Job Descriptions if Hiring Employees	
☐	Establish Your Business on Social Media	

Appendix

New Small Business Questionnaire

Use this business questionnaire if you are in the preliminary stages of starting a business or flushing out a business concept. It will help you to organize your thoughts and to better execute your next business venture.

SECTION A - *Established Business Details*

- ➢ I have a business **(Complete Sections A & C)**
- ➢ I don't have a business **(Complete Sections B & C)**

Business Name: _____ Years in Business: _____

What type of business do you have? Brick & Mortar or Online

Number of Business Partners: _____

Describe your business in 3-5 sentences.

_____

_____

_____

_____

Appendix

What products or services do you offer?

_____

_____

_____

_____

What's the one thing that's going extremely well in your business?

_____

_____

_____

_____

Why do you think that is?

_____

_____

Appendix

What are your top 3 challenges in your business?

Challenge #1:

How are you addressing it?

_____

_____

Challenge #2:

How are you addressing it?

_____

_____

Challenge #3:

How are you addressing it?

_____

_____

Appendix

Do you have a business plan?   Yes   No

Do you have an advisory board?   Yes   No

    If yes, how often do you meet? _____

How do you track your financials? _____

What are your YTD earnings for 20XX? _____

What are your projected earnings for 20XX? _____

How do you plan to increase revenue for 20XX? _____

_____

_____

_____

Do you have a logo?   Yes   No

    If no, find a graphic designer to create it for you. It should cost between $150-$350

Appendix

Do you have customized business cards with your logo?

      Yes   No

If no, do not print your business cards until you have a logo. Refer to chapter 1 for guidelines.

SECTION B – *New Business Details*

What 3 things are you most passionate about?

1. _____
2. _____
3. _____

Identify 3 things people always compliment you on or ask you to do?

1. _____
2. _____
3. _____

Appendix

What are your top 3 ideas for a business?

1. _____

2. _____

3. _____

What type of business do you want? Brick & Mortar - Online

How much would it cost to start? _____

Do you have money to start your idea business? Yes   No

Describe your ideal day as a business owner.

_____

_____

_____

_____

_____

Appendix

Define your idea of success.

_____

_____

_____

_____

Why do you want your own business?

_____

_____

_____

_____

_____

_____

Appendix

SECTION C - *Additional Business*

Social Media Platforms

     Instagram: _____

     Facebook: _____

     Twitter: _____

     Google+: _____

     Other: _____

Are you familiar with crowdfunding?
    Yes   No

If no, consider researching crowdfunding platforms like Kickstarter and Indiegogo to fund your next great idea.

If yes, have you ever used it to fund a project?
Yes   No

If yes, was the project a success?

Yes   No

Appendix

If yes, how much did you raise? _____

What made it successful or unsuccessful? What could you have done differently?

_____

_____

_____

_____

What are your top 3 goals for your business in the next 30-90 days?

Goal #1: _____

Goal #2: _____

Goal #3: _____

Appendix

What are your top 3 goals for your business in the next 90-120 days?

    Goal #1: _____

    Goal #2: _____

    Goal #3: _____

What are your top 3 goals for your business in the next 120-180 days?

    Goal #1: _____

    Goal #2: _____

    Goal #3: _____

Appendix

What are your top 3 goals for your business in the next year?

Goal #1: _____

Goal #2: _____

Goal #3: _____

Appendix

Appendix

BUILDING A BADASS BRAND WORKSHEETS

Key Definitions:

Branding - The process involved in creating a unique name and/or image for a product or service in the mind of the consumer. The goal of branding is to establish a significant and differentiated presence in the market that attracts and retains loyal customers.

Brand Benefits - Have a direct and immediate connection with the core user. The benefits accrue directly from the frame of reference. The brand benefits help differentiates you brand from your competition. They help establish the emotional connection and the brand advocacy between you and your consumers.

Brand Positioning Statement - Is a concise description of your target market as well as a compelling picture of how you want that market to perceive your brand. It is an internal tool designed to provide direction, focus and guidance both internally and externally. It clearly defines your purpose, function and how you will provide value to your consumers or

Appendix

customers. It is not your marketing program but it is the DNA from which your marketing, PR and advertising campaigns and strategies will be developed.

Core User - The core user is the pulse of your brand, they personify your brand and give it life. They help define the prestige, coolness factor or user imagery. When consumers see who really loves the brand it helps position the brand & enhance interest. If you were shooting a television commercial or positioning images for your website and wanted to highlight for your most loyal users, they are the people who would be in the commercial or featured on your website or print advertisement. If your consumers can't understand who or what you represent it is difficult for them to decide if they want to be associated with your brand.

Frame of Reference - The frame of reference establishes connection between your brand and is something your consumer can associate with. The frame of reference provides context to connect the benefits of your brand to your consumers. The frame of reference should always help position you from a point of strength.

Marketing - The process of moving goods and services from concept to consumer. It is the total activities involved from transfer of goods and services from producer or seller to consumer or buyer. It is the ongoing communications exchange with customers designed to educate, inform and stimulate purchase intent effectively done helps build relationships over time.

Appendix

Refer to Pages 90 -91 for key definitions

CORE USER

➢ Who is your core user?

_____
_____
_____
_____

➢ Who defines your brand?

_____
_____
_____
_____

➢ Who helps communicate the benefits of your products & services?

_____
_____
_____
_____

➢ If you shot an advertisement for your brand who would currently be in that commercial?

_____
_____
_____
_____

Appendix

Frame of Reference

The frame of reference establishes connection between your brand and is something your consumer can associate with. It should always help position you from a point of strength.

➢ The place where your brand will reside. (Ex: online, brick & mortar, etc.)

_____
_____
_____
_____
_____

➢ What description casts your brand, company or yourself in the most favorable light?

_____
_____
_____
_____
_____

Appendix

➢ What is the commonality exists between your competition and your brand?

_____
_____
_____
_____
_____

➢ How would you want your consumers to connect with your brand?

_____
_____
_____
_____
_____

Appendix

Brand Benefits

➢ What is unique about your brand (company or you)?

_____
_____
_____
_____

➢ What are the benefits or how does your core user win or gain advantage from using your brand (services)?

_____
_____
_____
_____

➢ Do your brand benefits have a direct and immediate connection with the core user?

_____
_____
_____
_____

➢ ***Point to remember:*** The benefits accrue directly from the frame of reference.

Appendix

➢ ***Point to remember:*** The brand benefit(s) helps differentiate the brand from competition.

➢ ***Point to remember:*** The brand benefits should help solidify the emotional connection between you and the core user.

Additional Brand Benefits Notes:

_____
_____
_____
_____
_____
_____
_____
_____
_____
_____
_____
_____
_____

Appendix

Your Positioning Statement

To......

_____
_____
_____
_____
_____
_____
_____

(Core User – Who best personifies your preferred user? This consumer provides the user imagery for your product.)

Brand X is the...

_____
_____
_____
_____
_____
_____
_____

(Frame of Reference – This is the context in which you want your consumer to think about your product or services.)

Appendix

That......

_____
_____
_____
_____
_____
_____
_____

(Brand Benefit – This is the direct benefit that your consumer will drive from using your product. This is where you strive to provide the emotional attachment.)

Your Positioning Elements Should Inlcude:

- Name:
  _____

- Formula:
  _____

- Packaging:
  _____
  _____

- Pricing:
  _____

Appendix

➢ Advertising:

➢ Distribution Channels:
-
-
-
-

➢ Consumer Promotions:

Appendix

- Trade Promotions:

  _____
  _____
  _____
  _____
  _____
  _____
  _____

- Publicity:

  _____
  _____
  _____
  _____
  _____
  _____

Evaluating Your Positioning Statement

- Is it memorable, motivating, and focused on the core user or desired prospect?   _____ **Yes**   _____ **No**

- Can the brand own it?   _____ **Yes**   _____ **No**

- Is it credible and believable? _____ **Yes**   _____ **No**

- Does it serve as a filter for brand decision making?

  _____ **Yes**   _____ **No**

Appendix

- Does your brand differentiate itself from other players in your category? _____ **Yes** _____ **No**

- Is your competitive positon likely to be defendable over time? _____ **Yes** _____ **No**

Index

Index

Angel Radcliffe	XIV,XV
Appendix	73
Brand Attributes	33
Brand Benefits	42,43
Brand Definition	32
Brand Equity	33
Brand Identity	33
Brand Image	33
Brand Promise	32
Build a Place Online To Do Business	10
Building a Badass Brand	31
Building a Badass Brand Worksheet	90
Building Business Credit	13
Building Customer Trust	51
Business Account	17
Business Apps	25
Business Structure	16
Bylaws	67
CamCard	28
Carla Jones	XII,XIII
Check your company's name	3
Client Acquisition	49
Collaborating	59
Common Objectives	61
Communication	53
Contact Management	27
Content Management	28
Core User	38,39
Create a Contract	64,66
Customer Care	55
Customer Satisfaction: It really does matter	55
Customer Relationship	51
DBA, Legal Business Name	18

Index

Defining your Audience	34
Defining What You Will Sacrifice to Own	36
Domain Name	4
Dun Number	18,19
Disbursements	62
Establish the Brand	9
Evernote	28
Exit Strategy	62
Expensify	26
Financial Management	26
Frame of Reference	40,41
Get insured	5
Homeowners Insurance	6
Ideal Audience	35
Incorporate your business	15
Introduction	VI
It's all about the Core User	38,39
It's not what you say, but how you say it	53
Insurance	5,6,7
Logo	8
Meetings	68
Members	68
Mileage	27
MileIQ	27
Name of Organization	67
New Business Checklist	75
New Business Questionnaire	78
Non-Disclosure Agreement (NDA)	64,65
Obtain a credit card or line of credit	22,23
Obtain a Duns Number	18,19
Officers	68
Open a business bank account	17
Open accounts with vendors and suppliers	20

Index

Positioning, How, Who and Why	43
Positioning Statement	33
Product Liability Insurance	7
Professional Liability Insurance	6
Property Insurance	6
Purpose	67
Sacrifice	36
Sealing the Deal with Clients	40
Secured Business Card	22
Smart Receipts	26
Table of Contents	V
Team Member Skills	63
Terré Holmes Arnold	X,XI
Timeframe	62
Vehicle Insurance	6
What Readers Are Saying	IV
Worker's Compensation Insurance	5

www.ingramcontent.com/pod-product-compliance
Lightning Source LLC
Chambersburg PA
CBHW021434170526
45164CB00001B/240